Teaching International Law

State-Consent as Consent to a Process of Normative Development and Ensuing Problems

Teaching International Law

State-Consent as Consent to a Process of Normative Development and Ensuing Problems

Ellen Hey

This text provided the basis for a lecture given by the author on accepting the Chair of Public International Law at the Faculty of Law of the Erasmus University Rotterdam on February 7, 2003

Published by:
Kluwer Law International
P.O. Box 85889, 2508 CN The Hague, The Netherlands
sales@kli.wkap.nl
http://www.kluwerlaw.com

Sold and Distributed in North, Central and South America by:
Kluwer Law International
101 Philip Drive, Norwell, MA 02061, USA
kluwerlaw@wkap.com

Sold and Distributed in all other countries by:
Kluwer Law International
Distribution Centre, P.O. Box 322, 3300 AH Dordrecht, The Netherlands

A CIP Catalogue record for this book is available from the Library of Congress

Printed on acid-free paper.

ISBN 90-411-2014-9

Painting on the front cover: Mi Desmedt, *Une Promenade dans la Campagne*
(for more information see inside back cover)

Typesetting and cover layout by *Steve Lambley Information Design*, The Hague

Kluwer Law International incorporates the publishing programmes of Graham & Trotman Ltd, Kluwer Law and Taxation Publishers and Martinus Nijhoff Publishers.

TEACHING INTERNATIONAL LAW

State-Consent as Consent to a Process of Normative Development and Ensuing Problems

When I was appointed to the Chair of Public International Law at the Faculty of Law of the Erasmus University Rotterdam, on May 1, 2002, my attention was unequivocally turned to teaching matters. Preparations for the introduction of the Bachelors/Masters structure into the regular curriculum were in process[1] and the curriculum for the LLM program in International Law was subject to evaluation.[2] Together these two developments raised questions about the content of the two curricula, the content of specific courses, but also about my approach to teaching international law in a globalizing world.

In considering the different courses and topics that I teach, I sought to develop a critical construct of the international legal system that offers students a basis for independent and further critical thinking about that system.[3] I soon realized that the concept of state-consent was to be pivotal in the story of the international legal system that I tell my students.[4] That story evolves around the changing concept of state-consent and the problems that arise as a result. The theme of that story is that state-consent, besides being understood as consent to a rule or a set of rules, increasingly is understood as consent to a process of normative development in the wake of which problems arise regarding the legitimacy of international decision-making processes.[5] It is this story that I share with you in this essay, which provided

---

1 For information on the regular curriculum see http://www.frg.eur.nl.

2 For information on the LLM programs see http://www.llm-erasmus.org/.

3 Dianne Otto, "Handmaidens, Hierarchies and Crossing the Public-Private Divide in the Teaching of International Law," 1 *Melbourne Journal of International Law* 2000, p. 35.

4 For an enlightening analysis of the concept of state-consent see O.A. Elias and C.L. Lim, *The Paradox of Consensualism in International Law*, Kluwer Law International, 1998.

the basis for my inaugural lecture in acceptance of the above-mentioned chair. I will consecutively consider the following topics: globalization and normative development, two types of normative patterns, the concept of state-consent as consent to a process of normative development and the problems that ensue when state-consent is understood in this manner.

Globalization and normative development

I consider globalization to be the process by which social relationships, including those of individuals and groups, extend across the globe.[6] Given currently available technology, I consider the process of globalization to be an inevitable process. I once stated it as follows.

> Its most salient manifestation probably is the increased ease with which individuals engage in transnational contacts – whether by way of the internet or phone, physical travel or the products that we buy in the corner-store. These contacts also have their 'flip side' – employees increasingly suffer from stress as a result of the around-the-clock economy, most forms of physical travel result in greenhouse gas emissions and the corner-store is fast disappearing. Most of us participate in the process of globalization – at least as consumers – and all of us may experience its effects ...[7]

Stating that social relationships extend across the globe means not only that you can buy a certain type of hamburger in many places across the world, but also that

---

[5] Many of my thoughts on the topic were inspired by the work of Jutta Brunnée and Stephen J. Toope on 'an interactional theory of international law' as reflected in Jutta Brunnée and Stephen J. Toope, "International Law and Constructivism: Elements of an Interactional Theory of International Law," 39 *Columbia Journal of Transnational Law* 2000, p. 19, by the same authers, "Interactional International Law," 3 *International Law FORUM du Droit International* 2001, p. 186 as well as other articles by the same authors referred to in this essay. The references to 'problems and process' was inspired by the title of Rosalyn Higgins's book *Problems & Process, International Law and How We Use It*, Clarendon Press, 1994.

[6] For further insights into the nature of the process of globalization see Ulrich Beck, *What is Globalization?*, Polity Press, 2000.

[7] Ellen Hey, "Globalization and International Organizations," introduction to the 'Recurring Themes' column, 2 *International Law FORUM du Droit International* 2000, p. 220, at p. 220, also see by the same author, "Globalization and International Law," introduction to the 'Recurring Themes' column, 4 *International Law FORUM du Droit International* 2002, p. 12.

intellectual, moral, legal and political discourse need no longer be limited by your geographical location. The latter, the worldwide nature of political, legal, moral and intellectual discourse, implies that society is constituting itself at the transnational or global level, a process in which international law plays an important role.[8] While this self-constituting process, for example, has contributed to a high degree of consensus emerging about the indivisibility of civil and political rights and social, cultural and economic rights,[9] the process is ongoing and its outcomes are uncertain.

One of the effects of the process of globalization has been that increasingly decisions are taken at the regional and international level. This development in turn has resulted in individuals and groups that perceive their interests as being affected by those decisions, demanding participation in the decision-making processes at the regional and international level. The wide-spread participation of non-governmental organizations as observers in international conferences and in their own meetings parallel to those conferences are an outcome of this demand. Concomitantly, questions regarding the legitimacy and accountability of non-governmental organizations have arisen.[10] Moreover, the continuously ongoing decision-making processes in international governmental organizations and treaty-based bodies have resulted in these organizations increasingly being perceived as taking on roles that were not foreseen when the organizations were established and in the fulfillment of which they often act with a degree of independence from their member states. This development in turn has raised questions regarding the legitimacy and in particular the accountability of these forums.[11]

---

8 See Philip Allott, "The Concept of International Law," 10 *European Journal of International Law* 1999, p. 31.

9 This consensus is reflected in, among other documents, the *Vienna Declaration and Programme of Action*, UN Doc. A/CONF. 157/23, 12 July 1993, adopted by the World Conference on Human Rights, Vienna 14-25 June 1993, See, in particular para 5.

10 See for example, Hilary Charlesworth and Christine Chinkin, *The Boundaries of International Law, A Feminist Analysis*, Manchester University Press, 2000, pp. 88-93; Humanitarian Accountability Project (HAP), *The Accountable Organisation*, HAP Index ACC/20/03/2002, 20 March 2002, http://www.hapgeneva.org. More generally on the role of non-state actors see *Proceedings of the 92nd Annual Meeting of the American Society of International Law*, 1998, p. 380; Bas Arts, Math Noortmann and Bob Reinalda (eds.), *Non-State Actors in International Relations*, Ashgate, 2001.

11 See, for example, Dan Bodansky, "The Legitimacy of International Governance: A Coming Challenge for International Environmental Law?," 93 *American Journal of International Law* 1999, p. 596; Jutta Brunnée, "COPing with Consent: Law-Making Under Multilateral Environmental Agreements," 15 *Leiden Journal of International Law* 2002, p. 1; Outi Korhonene, "International Governance in Post-Conflict Situations," 14 *Leiden Journal of International Law* 2001, p. 495; Sundhya Pahuja, "Technologies of Empire: IMF Conditionality

While many individuals and groups remain excluded from the transnational debate, as they do from buying the products generated as a result of the globalization of the economy, they are nevertheless participants in the process of globalization. Think of the farmers in developing countries who, among other things, as a result of subsidies to agricultural exports in, for example, the European Union and the United States are prevented from producing economically viable food products for their home market, with hungry and even starving populations as a result.[12] Think of international arms sales and the millions of refugees living in deprived conditions, who have fled their home-countries because of armed conflicts that threaten their livelihood and lives.[13] Think of the victims of the attacks of September 11, 2001 and the global scene in which the perpetrators operated.[14] These individuals – the farmer, the hungry, the refugee and the victim of terrorist actions – are undergoing the effects of globalization, effects that are not to their benefit. These individuals are not excluded from the process of globalization, they are participants in the process and globalization, in some cases, is resulting in their marginalization.

What the above-mentioned examples illustrate is that social relationships increasingly are transnational or global in nature. That is, social links have been established between individuals, states, international governmental organizations, transnational corporations and non-governmental organizations and in those links national and

---

and the Reinscription of the North/South Divide," 13 *Leiden Journal of International Law* 2000, p. 749; Bimal N. Patel, "The Accountability of International Organisations: Case Study of the Organisation for the Prohibition of Chemical Weapons," 13 *Leiden Journal of International Law* 2000, p. 571; see also consideration of the topic at the at the Annual Meeting of the American Society of International Law (ASIL) in 1998 and 2000 (resp. ASIL Proceedings of the 92nd Annual Meeting, 1998, p. 359 and ASIL Proceedings of the 94th Annual Meeting, 2000, p. 204); International Law Association's Committee on the Accountability of International Organizations, Second Report, International Law Association, *Report of the Sixty-Ninth Conference*, 2000, p. 875. The International Law Commission has also commenced work on the topic 'responsibility of international organizations', *Report of the International Law Commission to General Assembly*, 54th session, Official Record General Assembly, 57 session, Supplement No.10(A/57/10), 2002, p. 228.

12 Marcel Mazoyer, *Protecting Small Farmers and the Rural Poor in the Context of Globalization*, FAO, 2001, also see para. 12 of the Declaration of the World Food Summit: Five Years Later, adopted at the World Food Summit, June 2002. Both documents are available from the website of the FAO http://www.fao.org.

13 ICRC, *Arms Availability and the Situation of Civilians in Armed Conflict*, 1999, available form the website of the International Committee of the Red Cross http://www/icrc.org.

14 Antonio Cassese, "Terrorism is also Disrupting Some Crucial Categories of International Law," 12 *European Journal of International Law* 2001, p. 993.

geographic boundaries play an increasingly insignificant role. With the intensification of transnational social relationships, increasingly forces are in place that seek to translate these social relationships into legal relationships. In this endeavor we are trying to address the consequences of globalization, including marginalization. Moreover, we are seeking to develop legal relationships that address issues of concern to the international community as a whole and that, in addition to states, directly involve individuals, groups – be they, for example, non-governmental organizations, indigenous peoples or transnational corporations – and international organizations.

Given the inter-state nature of the traditional international legal system and its focus on the shared interests of states, efforts to develop legal relationships involving entities other than states and that seek to address community interests entail the introduction of systemic change into the existing international legal system. In other words, the inter-state nature of the current international legal system entails that that system is ill-equipped to translate social relationships that are arising as a result of globalization into legal relationships.

Introducing systemic change into a legal system is a cumbersome endeavor. It is fraught with uncertainties and meets with opposition from those with vested interests in the existing system – often including those educated in that system, in our case international lawyers. Such opposition, while it may delay or even prevent legal development, in many cases does not prevent normative development. In other words, such opposition will not prevent the translation of social relationships in terms of normative relationships nor prevent the development of normative systems that have characteristics of a legal system, but that remain short of qualifying as public international law in the traditional sense because they do not fit the definition of law in that system.[15] As a result of this development, situations of normative pluralism arise.[16] The existence of normative systems outside the official state-made

[15] For an analysis of this situation see Charlesworth and Chinkin, *supra* note 10, pp. 62-95; G.J. van Hoof, *Rethinking the Sources of International Law*, Kluwer, 1983.

[16] Keebet von Benda-Beckmann, "Globalisation and Legal Pluralism," 4 *International Law FORUM du Droit International* 2002, p. 19; Gunther Teubner, "'Global Bukowina': Legal Pluralism in the World Society," Gunther Teubner (ed.), *Global Law without a State*, Dartmouth, 1997, p. 3.

international legal system and discussions regarding the nature and status of such normative systems, however, are not new. The long-standing discussion regarding the nature and status of *lex mercatoria* offers an example.[17]

What we currently are witnessing at the international level of decision-making under the influence of the process of globalization are attempts to translate transnational social relationships into transnational normative relationships, with some of these normative relationships being accommodated into the current legal system, while others remain outside or at the borders of that system. As a result of this ongoing process, the international legal system is undergoing continuous systemic change, with the concept of state-consent changing in the process.

I capture this situation of ongoing systemic change in terms of telling my students the story of the international legal system based on two normative patterns – the inter-state normative pattern and the common-interest normative pattern, with state-consent playing a distinct role in each pattern. I am indebted to Antonio Cassese for his reference to these two patterns, albeit in slightly different terms. Cassese refers to the patterns as the old and new, the traditional and modern or the 'Grotian' and the 'Kantian' patterns of international law to tell students his story of *International Law*.[18] Precursors, however, exist; most prominent are the twin concepts of the law of co-existence and the law of cooperation developed by Wolfgang Freedman,[19] concepts that have found their way into many a textbook.[20] Other textbooks refer to attempts to develop universal law and the problems encountered *en route*.[21]

---

17 Hans-Joachim Mertens, "*Lex Mercatoria*: A Self-applying System Beyond National Law?," in Teubner (ed.), *supra* note 16, p. 31; Jean-Phillippe Robé, "Multinational Enterprises: The Constitution of a Pluralistic Legal Order," in the same volume, p. 45.

18 Antonio Cassese, *International Law*, Oxford University Press, 2001. See p. 18 of the book for a short summary of the two models.

19 Wolfgang Freedman, *The Changing Structure of International Law*, Stevens & Sons, 1964.

20 For example, P.H. Kooijmans, *Internationaal Publiekrecht in Vogelvlucht* (Public International Law, a Birdseye View), W.J. Tjeenk Willink, 8th edition, 2000.

21 Peter Malanczuk, *Akehurst's Modern Introduction to International Law*, 7th revised edition, Routledge, 1997, esp. at pp. 30-31 and 37-38.

Two types of normative patterns

I tell my students that, besides self-regulatory normative patterns, such as *lex mercatoria*,[22] two main types of normative patterns can be distinguished at the international level. As stated above, I refer to these patterns as the inter-state normative pattern and the common-interest normative pattern. The first pattern defines social relationships between states in terms of what is traditionally considered to be public international law. The second pattern defines social relationships between states as well as other actors both in terms of what is traditionally considered to be public international law and in terms of normative systems that are not traditionally considered to be part of public international law. Normative development in the second pattern includes state-made law as well as normative development within international organizations and treaty-based bodies. Examples of the former are the internal rules and regulations adopted by development banks, such as the World Bank,[23] and of the latter the decisions adopted by the Conference of the Parties to the United Nations Framework Convention on Climate Change.[24] These types of decisions are considered to be relevant to public international law, but generally as such are not considered to be legally binding in that system because states have not agreed to award them that status. In other words, state-consent is lacking.

I also tell my students that where the two patterns meet difficulties and uncertainties usually arise. A pertinent example is the decision of the International Court of Justice in the *Arrest Warrant* case.[25] In that case, the law on immunities, belonging to the inter-state normative pattern, and the law on serious violations of international humanitarian law, belonging to the common-interest normative pattern, were at stake. Yet the majority of the Court, helped by the reformulation of the

---

22 See references in *supra* note 17.

23 See Günther Handl, "The Mandate of Multilateral Development Banks as Agents for Change Toward Sustainable Development," 92 *American Journal of International Law* 1998, p. 642; Benedict Kingsbury, "Operational Policies of International Institutions as Part of the Law-Making Process: The World Bank and Indigenous Peoples," in Guy S. Goodwin-Gill and Stefan Talmon (eds.), *The Reality of International Law, Essays in Honour of Ian Brownlie*, 1999, p. 323.

24 See Brunnée, *supra* note 11, also see Robin R. Churchill and Geir Ulfstein, "Autonomous Institutional Arrangements in Multilateral Environmental Agreements: A Little Noticed Phenomenon in International Law," 94 *American Journal of International Law* 2000, p. 623.

25 ICJ, *Case Concerning the Arrest Warrant of 11 April 2000* (Democratic Republic of Congo v. Belgium), 14 February 2002, General List 121.

questions put to it by the appellant, found it unnecessary to address the relationships between these two bodies of law.[26] The result is continuing uncertainty about that relationship.

The actions of the United States *vis-á-vis* the International Criminal Court provide a second example of the inter-state and common-interest normative patterns meeting.[27] The problem concerns the fact that the jurisdiction of the International Criminal Court may encompass US citizens even if the United States is not a party to the Statute of the International Criminal Court – typical of the common-interest normative pattern.[28] As a result of this situation, the United States, in order to avoid its nationals being subjected to the jurisdiction of the Court, has concluded agreements with other states on the non-surrender of their nationals to the International Criminal Court – typical of the inter-state normative pattern.[29] Interesting in this respect,

---

[26] In its original application Congo had contested both the exercise of universal jurisdiction by Belgium and the non-recognition by Belgium of the immunity of the Congolese Foreign Minister (para. 17). However, in the submissions in its Memorial and in its final submissions Congo submitted only the latter point (para. 21). This amendment of the submissions, according to the judgment, justifies the approach adopted by the Court. That is, to 'address first the question whether, assuming that Belgium had jurisdiction under international law to issue and circulate the arrest warrant of 11 April 2000, Belgium in so doing violated the immunities of the then Minister of Foreign Affairs of the Congo' (para. 46). Most Judges in their opinions commented on this approach and some suggest that, as a point of logic, the Court should have first considered the question of whether Belgium was entitled to exercise jurisdiction, regardless of whether the appellant had submitted that question to the Court or not. The variety of opinions submitted by the different judges, however, reflects the difficulties and uncertainties that the Court faced in considering the relationship between these two areas of law.

[27] Frédèric Mégret, "Epilogue to an Endless Debate: The International Criminal Debate: The International Criminal Court's Third Party Jurisdiction and the Looming Revolution in International Law," 12 *European Journal of International Law* 2001, p. 247.

[28] Under article 13(a) and (c) *junto* article 12(2) of its Statute International Criminal Court may exercise jurisdiction if either the state in which the conduct occurred or the state of nationality if the suspect is a party to the Statute. Furthermore, under article 13(b) it may also exercise jurisdiction of the United Nations Security Council acting under Chapter VII of the Charter refers a case to the Prosecutor. In that case the requirements set out in article 12(2) do not apply.

[29] For information and the text of, so-called, 'article 98 agreements' see the website of the Campaign to End Genocide, http://www.endgenocide.org. On November 14 the United States had conclude such agreements with 14 countries: Afghanistan, the Dominican Republic (s), East Timor (r), EL Salvador, the Gambia (r), The Gambia, Honduras (r), Israel (s and announced it will not ratify, nor accept any obligations), the Marshall Islands (r), Mauritania, Micronesia, Palau, Romania (r), Tajikistan (r) and Uzbekistan (s). Six of these states are parties to (indicated by (r)) and three states have signed (indicated by (s)) the Statute of the International Criminal Court. Romania and East Timor have announced that the agreements concluded with the United States require the approval of their parliaments to enter into force

is that the United States also used a common-interest mechanism – a resolution of the Security Council[30] – to attain the same aim. I will return to this example towards the end of this essay.

I also tell my students that the process of change towards including the common-interest normative pattern in public international law is gradual. Moreover, I share with them the proviso, that the common-interest normative pattern, as the inter-state normative pattern, is the outcome of a political process in which states and other actors pursue their real or perceived interests. In other words, intrinsically 'good' or 'bad' normative systems are not at stake, but rather normative patterns through which relevant actors seek to translate social relationships into legal relationships.

The inter-state normative pattern

The inter-state normative pattern defines legal relationships between states and seeks to regulate those interests that states share, as opposed to the common interests of the international community. Its origins are generally traced to the Peace of Westphalia, concluded in 1648, and the nascent inter-state system established at the time.[31] A typical example of this pattern of law is the law on state and diplomatic immunities.[32] The most manifest expression of the inter-state paradigm is the concept of state-consent. That concept within the inter-state normative pattern implies that a state cannot be bound by a rule of public international law unless it has consented, expressly or tacitly, to that rule. The inter-state pattern of law might thus be characterized as law for states that is made by states and that is applicable to an individual state only if that state has consented to the law in question.[33] As a result, the inter-state pattern can also be characterized as reciprocal in nature and as a pattern of law

(Information obtained from the above mentioned website and from the website of the ICC http://www.un.org/law/icc.).

30 UNSC Resolution 1422 (2002), 12 July 2002, UN. Doc. S/Res/1422 (2002).

31 See, for example Cassese, *supra* note 18, p. 19 and following.

32 Vienna Convention on Diplomatic Relations, 16 April 1961, 500 UNTS 95.

33 See generally, Ko Swan Sik, *De Verplichting in het Volkenrecht* (The Obligation in Public International Law), T.M.C. Asser Institute, 1990, Inaugural lecture on acceptance of the Chair of Public International Law at the Erasmus University Rotterdam, June 22, 1990,

that is in fact more akin to what in national law is known as private law than to national administrative or public law.[34]

The concept of state-consent in the inter-state normative pattern results, for example, in the somewhat strange situation that even in the case of a multilateral treaty, the treaty in fact defines bilateral legal relationships between the different states-parties to the treaty. This situation can be illustrated with reference to the rules on reservations as contained in the Vienna Convention on the Law of Treaties.[35] Those rules determine that, except in the case of a reservation against the object and purpose of the treaty – an ever-contentious concept[36] – the content of the legal relationship between any two parties to a multilateral treaty is determined by the content of the reservation and the reaction thereto by another state-party.[37] This situation has resulted in the inclusion of a provision prohibiting reservations in many multilateral treaties that deal with common-interest problems, such as, for example, multilateral environmental treaties.[38]

The inter-state normative pattern is the most evident pattern if we consider textbooks on public international law. Many textbooks adopt the following pattern in their exposé of the subject matter: the presentation of a rule or point of departure of public international law, followed by a long list of exceptions, with each exception being exceptional in its own right and requiring lengthy explanation. I provide you with one example of how a typical textbook explanation is constructed. I have omitted the lengthy explanations of the exceptions, as those explanations would take up the rest of the space available for this essay.

> *The main subjects of public international law are states. They make the law, which applies to them. Exceptions to this rule are international organizations as evidenced by, among other decisions, the*

---

34 H. Lauterpacht, *Private Law Sources and Analogies of International Law (with special reference to arbitration)*, Longmans, Green and Co., 1927.

35 See articles 19 through 22, Vienna Convention on the Law of Treaties, 1155 UNTS 331.

36 Isabelle Buffard and Karl Zemanek, "The 'Object and Purpose' of a Treaty: An Enigma?," 3 *Austrian Review of International Law & European Law* 1998, p. 311; Jan Klabbers, "Some Problems Regarding the Object and Purpose of Treaties," 8 *Finnish Yearbook of International Law* 1997, p. 138.

37 Art. 21, Vienna Convention on the Law of Treaties.

38 See, for example, art. 24 of the United Nations Framework Convention on Climate Change, 31 *International Legal Materials* (ILM) 1992, p. 849 and art. 37 of the Convention on Biological Diversity, 31 ILM 818 (1992).

advisory opinion in Reparations for Injuries,[39] *and individuals in human rights law and international criminal law. In addition, insurgents, national liberation movements, minorities and indigenous peoples have a special status under international law. Furthermore, there are older examples of exceptions to this basic rule. Most noteworthy among these exceptions are, pirates, the Holy See and the International Committee of the Red Cross. Moreover, there is an ongoing debate as to whether multinational corporations might in certain cases be regarded as holding rights and duties under international law.*

This approach – the rule, numerous exceptions and lengthy explanation of exceptions – can be explained and is also to some extent justified by the fact that in teaching any subject, especially at less advanced levels, we are usually engaged in constructing a system for our students, a system that enables them to define categories and relationships between those categories. The inter-state pattern of international law offers just that: a systematic construct for our story of public international law. However, I contend that this construct has become too far removed from contemporary normative development at the transnational level; it is a part of but it is not the full story of the international legal system that I tell my students.

The common-interest normative pattern

The common-interest normative pattern defines legal relationships between a variety of actors that operate at the transnational level. It seeks to regulate the interests that are common to these actors or the interests of the international community. States play an important role in this system; however, other actors also figure prominently. Although predecessors can be identified, this pattern started to manifest itself after the First World War and in particular after the Second World War, most notably through the establishment of international organizations, attempts to ban the use of force and the development of human rights law.[40] As a result of these developments, concepts such as that of the international community, the common or community interest and obligations *erga omnes* gained ground.[41] A typical example of this second

[39] See *infra* note 51.

[40] See Cassese, *supra* note 18, page 30 and following.

[41] See Mauricio Ragazzi, *The Concept of Obligations* Erga Omens, Clarendon Press, 1997; Brunno Simma, "From Bilateralism to Community Interest in International Law," 250 *Recueil des Cours* 1994-VI, p. 221.

normative pattern is international criminal law.[42] State-consent also plays an important role in many manifestations of this normative pattern. However, in this normative pattern, state-consent often is best understood as consent to a process, rather than consent to a rule. This pattern of normative development is more akin to what in national law is captured under the term public law.

Developing the common-interest normative pattern is fraught with difficulties because it involves introducing systemic change into the inter-state normative pattern. To put it otherwise, it involves changing the rules of the game, or, in the terms used by Hart, it involves changing the secondary rules of the inter-state normative pattern, in addition to changing the primary or substantive rules of international law.[43] Moreover, as a specific secondary rule is altered, new problems manifest themselves, which may require further changes in both the primary and secondary rules. A pertinent example is the following: when state-consent is understood as consent to a process of normative development, issues related to the legitimacy of the decision-making process arise because most decision-making processes at the international level reflect the inter-state normative pattern and thus are not attuned to the common-interest normative pattern. The process of change is many-faceted and ongoing and presents us, among other things, with demands for change in the decision-making process. The story of the international legal system that I tell my students includes these issues, not as exceptions to a rule, but rather as manifestations of a diverse and multi-centered norm-making process, a process that often raises problems, which in turn give rise to new processes and problems. In the rest of this essay I will address the changing perception of the concept of state-consent as well as some of the problems and further processes that this changing perception is giving rise to.

State-consent as consent to a process of normative development

At first sight, the concept of the common interest and state-consent appear to be uneasy partners. That assessment is correct if the traditional understanding of state-consent is adopted. In that understanding, state-consent is portrayed as consent to a

[42] Cassese, "The Statute of the International Criminal Court : Some Preliminary Reflections," 10 *European Journal of International Law* 1999, p.144; Mégret, *supra* note 27.

[43] H.L.A. Hart, *The Concept of Law*, Oxford University Press, 1961, reprint Clarendon Press, 1993.

rule or to, at most, a set of rules in the form of a treaty. A different perspective, however, emerges if state-consent is understood as consent to a process of normative development, the outcome of which is undetermined at the time at which that consent is given. The aim of the process might be characterized as the translation of social relationships into normative, including legal, relationships. In other words, by giving their consent to an instrument, usually an initial treaty, that involves the common interest, states agree to participate in and accept the outcome of a process aimed at normative development. The resulting normative development may include manifestations that qualify as law under the traditional definition of public international law, but it also may include normative developments that do not qualify as such because they do not fit the definition of what is traditionally considered to be public international law. Examples of this process are decisions of the Human Rights Committee related to individual complaints submitted under the Covenant on Civil and Political Rights and rulings of the European Court of Human Rights related to similar complaints submitted under the European Convention on Human Rights. The former are legally non-binding, the latter are legally binding, and both are part of the common-interest pattern of normative development.

A manifestation of the common-interest normative pattern is the decision of the International Court of Justice in the *Gabčikovo-Nagymaros* case.[44] In that case the Court decided that the provisions on the protection of the environment contained in a bilateral treaty concluded in 1977 contained 'evolving provisions', which enable the incorporation of new environmental norms into the process by which the treaty is implemented and that the responsibility to do so was the joint responsibility of the two states.[45] It is noteworthy that this case, on the face of it, concerned a bilateral dispute only. The Court, however, found 'the very health of human beings, including generations unborn' to be at stake when it came to the duty of the two states to cooperate in order to protect the environment.[46] What but the common or community interest and an obligation *erga omnes* could this reference be to?[47] In terms of

---

[44] ICJ, case *Concerning the Gabčikovo-Nagymaros Project* (Hungary v. Slovakia), 25 September 1997, ICJ Reports 1997.

[45] Para. 112, *Gabčikovo-Nagymaros*.

[46] Id. and paragraph 53, where the Court quotes from its Advisory Opinion on the *Legality of the Threat or Use of Nuclear Weapons* ICJ reports 1996, para. 29.

[47] See A.E. Boyle, "The *Gabčikovc-Nagymaros* Case: New Law in Old Bottles," 8 *Yearbook of International Environmental Law* 1997, p. 13.

state-consent as consent to a process, the case might well be understood as follows. The two states Hungary and Slovakia, the later as the successor state to Czechoslovakia, by way of the 'evolving provisions', had in 1977 agreed to include in the implementation of the Treaty, the then unknown outcome of a multilateral process for the development of international environmental law – part of the common-interest normative pattern.

The United Nations Convention on the Law of the Sea[48] (LOS Convention) also illustrates how state-consent as consent to a process of normative development has been incorporated into a multilateral treaty. The LOS Convention contains what are often referred to as rules of reference. These rules are provisions that refer to parties having the duty to take into account or apply "internationally agreed rules, standards and recommended practices and procedures" or "generally accepted international rules and standards established through the competent international organization or general diplomatic conference".[49] It is generally agreed that this reference is to rules and standards that may be adopted after the LOS Convention entered into force and that such rules and standards may be included in both legally binding and legally non-binding instruments. Moreover, such rules and standards may be adopted within international organizations, such as the International Maritime Organization, and through treaties. While a host of questions may and have been posed regarding the legal effect of such provisions,[50] these provisions entail that a party to the LOS Convention consents not only to rules contained in that convention, but also to a process or processes for further developing rules and standards and to the rules and standards resulting from these processes.

State-consent as consent to a process of normative development, however, is not as new as the above-mentioned examples may lead one to believe. The 1949 advisory opinion of the International Court of Justice in *Reparation for Injuries*[51] and the fact that the Court in that case found state-consent to provide the basis for the 'implied powers' doctrine, provide an early example of this development. The Court

---

48 21 *ILM* 1261 (1982).

49 See, respectively, arts. 207(1) and 211(2).

50 International Law Association Committee on Coastal State Jurisdiction Relating to Marine Pollution, Second Report, 1998, International Law Association, *Report of the Sixty-Eighth Conference*, 1998, p. 372; E.J. Molenaar, *Coastal State Jurisdiction over Vessel-Source Pollution*, Kluwer Law International, 1998.

51 ICJ, *Reparation for Injuries Suffered in the Service of the United Nations*, April 11, 1949, ICJ Rep. 1949.

at various places refers to the intentions of its founders, powers conferred on the organization and to practice that confirmed the character of the organization and that was supported, or at least not countered, by the member states. The Court refers to the rights and duties of the organization as dependent on 'its purposes and functions as specified and implied in its constituent documents and *developed in practice*' (emphasis added).[52] What the Court in fact seems to be saying is that, by becoming a party to the United Nations Charter, states agreed to participate in a process of normative development on the basis of the Charter. The outcome of that process allows the Court to conclude that the United Nations has legal personality on the international plane and is entitled to exercise diplomatic protection on behalf of its employees, even if the Charter or related documents did not explicitly provide for such powers.

A similar development can be detected in human rights law. In this case the concept is emerging that a third party may play a decisive role in determining the validity of reservations made to a human rights treaty. The discourse on the relationship between the law on reservations, typical of the inter-state normative pattern, and human rights law, typical of the common-interest normative patter, however, dates back to the 1951 advisory opinion of the International Court of Justice in *Reservations to Genocide*.[53] In *Reservations to Genocide*, the International Court of Justice found that the principles underlying the Genocide Convention and the universal character of the condemnation of genocide justified the conclusion that the General Assembly and the parties intended the convention to have a universal scope.[54] This intention, according to the Court, meant that as wide a participation in the convention as possible should be facilitated, which in turn, according to the Court, meant that such participation should not be hampered by the then contemporary law on reservations.[55] Furthermore the Court found that such an approach was justified by the 'purely humanitarian and civilizing purpose' of the convention, a convention in

52 Page 180, *Reparations for Injuries*.

53 ICJ, *Reservations to the Convention on the Prevention and Punishment of the Crime of Genocide*, May 28, 1951, ICJ Reports 1951.

54 Page 23, *Reservations to Genocide*.

55 The then relevant rules on reservation entailed that a reservation to a multilateral treaty was only valid if it was accepted by all states parties to the treaty. As a consequence, a state that wished to make a reservation to a multilateral treaty could not become a party thereto unless all other states parties accepted its reservation.

which 'the contracting States do not have any interest of their own; they merely have, one and all, *a common interest*' (emphasis added).[56] This reasoning resulted in the alteration by the court of the then contemporary rules on reservations to treaties for purposes of the Genocide Convention, and eventually in those new rules being incorporated in the Vienna Convention on the Law of Treaties and attaining general validity.[57] The confrontation between the old and new patterns, or between the law on reservations and human rights law, however, did not end there.

Recently the International Law Commission has been considering the topic of reservations to treaties.[58] Despite the conclusion that the Vienna Convention's articles on reservation do not require amendment in general or in respect of human rights or other normative treaties, it is clear from the work of the International Law Commission on the topic of reservations to treaties that human rights treaties and other normative treaties have a special character.[59] However, human rights treaties and other normative treaties are not considered to be special enough to merit special treatment in the guidelines that the International Law Commission will develop. The special position of these treaties, instead, according to the International Law Commission, is to be dealt with elsewhere, in the regimes provided by the human rights treaties themselves, by way of monitoring bodies established

---

[56] Page 23, *Reservations to Genocide*.

[57] See *supra* note 35. The articles in the Vienna Convention on the Law of Treaties maintain this situation where reservations that are contrary to the object and purpose of the treaty are concerned. With respect to other reservation, state parties to a multilateral convention may either accept or reject a reservation, thereby determining the content of the legal relationship between the reserving state and the state accepting or rejecting the reservation and giving rise to the situation where different legal relationships may exist between the different parties to a multilateral treaty.

[58] See, Alain Pellet, Special Rapporteur, Seventh Report on Reservations to Treaties, August 2002, UN Doc. A.CN.4/526, available from the website of the International Law Commission http://www.un.org/law/ilc. From paragraph 48 onwards the report considers the practice under certain human rights treaties.

[59] See in particular the Second Report of the Special Rapporteur on the topic, Alain Pellet, and especially its 2nd chapter, entitled "Unity or diversity of the legal regime for reservations to treaties", with the subtitle "reservations to human rights treaties" UN Doc. A/CN.4/477/Add.1, paras 55-260. Also relevant are the Preliminary Conclusions of the International Law Commission in Reservations to Normative Multilateral Treaties Including Human Rights Treaties, adopted by the International Law Commission following the consideration of the aforementioned report by the Special Rapporteur. For the text of the Preliminary Conclusion see para. 157, *Report of the ILC on its 49th session, Official Records of the General Assembly, 52nd session, Supplement No. 1(A/52/10), part C* (Hereinafter Preliminary Conclusions).

by those treaties.[60] It is in this respect interesting to note that the International Law Commission states that where such bodies have been established and the treaties remain silent on their competence to comment on the admissibility of reservations, such commissions are competent to engage in such comments.[61] It also notes that the legal force of any findings cannot exceed the powers allocated to such a body.[62] Although the final word about reservations to human rights treaties certainly has not been said,[63] the findings of the International Law Commission, and in particular those that endorse existing practice in the absence of explicit treaty provisions, do result in loosening the concept of state-consent.[64] This loosening of the concept of state-consent can be regarded as entailing a revision of the concept of state-consent in terms of consent to a process of normative development, rather than to rules or a set of rules. The practice of human rights bodies is illustrative.

In this respect two issues are of interest. First I will consider the approach adopted by several human rights bodies that operate under specific treaties. Most of these bodies comment on the compatibility of reservations with the object and purpose of the convention in question and subsequently engage the state in question in a dialogue the object of which is to obtain the withdrawal of the reservation.[65] These bodies arguably have instituted a process in which states consent to participate by virtue of their consent to the treaty in question. Moreover, the aim of that process is to reduce the reservations to the instrument in question and thus to foster normative development. The Human Rights Committee, however, has adopted a different approach, in which it does not apply the previous consideration to those reservations that it considers to be not in conformity with the object and purpose of the Covenant on Civil and Political Rights and the First Optional Protocol. It instead proceeds to comment on such reservations and sets them aside in the consideration

---

60 See Preliminary Conclusions.

61 Paragraph 5, Preliminary Conclusions.

62 Paragraph 8, Preliminary Conclusions.

63 In paragraph 55 of his seventh report, *supra* note 58, Pellet indicates that it might be useful for the International Law Commission to re-examine its Preliminary Conclusions in one or two years' time.

64 See the text at and *infra* notes 65-67.

65 *Supra* note 58 and, for example the practice of the Committee on the Elimination of Discrimination against Women regarding reservations as set out on the website of the UN Division for the Advancement of Women, http://www.un.org/womenwatch/daw/cedaw/reservations.

of individual complaints submitted to it, albeit in legally non-binding terms.[66] Although there is opposition to the manner in which human rights bodies, and in particular the Human Rights Committee, have proceeded, the International Law Commission apparently accepts this working method based on the concept that states, by giving their consent to the treaty in question, have consented to the procedure developed by the human rights body in question.

A second noteworthy development is the reasoning adopted by the European Court of Human Rights, when considering the legality of reservations. The European Court of Human Rights systematically states that the main intention of a party upon ratification of an instrument – Convention or Protocol – is its intention to be bound by the instrument in question, and also to be so bound if a reservation is found to be invalid.[67] That main intention, according to the European Court of Human Rights, is to prevail due to the special character of the Convention as an instrument of European public order. That then leads the Court to conclude that the main intention of the party remains and rules, even if the Court declares a reservation by that party to be invalid. On the basis of this argument the Court does two things. First, it sets aside or at least modifies the rules on reservations as contained in the Vienna Convention on the Law of Treaties. Second, it concludes that the state in question, when becoming a party to the Convention, has agreed not only to the provisions in the Convention, but also to a process of legal development in which the Court plays a pivotal role. This role entitles the Court to modify what were thought to be the applicable rules, in this case on reservations, with reference to the

---

66 See General Comment 24, *Issues relating to reservations made upon ratification or accession to the Covenant or the Optional Protocols thereto, or in relation to declarations under article 41 of the Covenant*, adopted by the Human Rights Committee at its fifty-second session, 1994, available from the website of the Office of the High Commissioner for Human Rights, http://www.unhchr.ch. Also see comments Human Rights Committee on the reservation made by the United States to art 6 (death penalty). Furthermore, see Human Rights Committee, Communication No. 845/1999: Trinidad and Tobago, UN Doc CCPR/C/67/D/845/1999, 31 December 1999. In this Communication the Human Rights Committee proceeded to determine that a reservation made by Trinidad and Tobago to the Optional Protocol to the effect that the Human Rights Committee would not be entitled to receive and consider communications relating to any prisoner under sentence of death was contrary to the object and purpose of the Optional Protocol and thus did not preclude the Committee from considering the communication in question.

67 See ECHR, *Belilos* case 1988, Series A, no. 132 (1988), para 60; *Weber* case, 1990, Series A, no. 177 (1990), paras. 38-40, *Loizidou* (preliminary objections), 1995, Series A, no. 310 (1995), paras. 90-98, available from the website of the ECHR http://www.echr.coe.int.

public order, or to put it in the terms that I have used in this essay, the common interest.

The above-mentioned examples are particularly salient ones where the concept of state-consent seems to be understood as consent to a process, rather than consent to a rule or set of rules. However, similar considerations arise with respect to decisions taken by other international organizations or organs established by multilateral treaties.[68]

Consent to a process of normative development and ensuing problems

The concept of state-consent as consent to a process of normative development is not unproblematic in international law. As state-consent is changing from being perceived as consent to a rule to consent to a process of normative development, questions arise related to the legitimacy and transparency of that process and about the accountability of the international organizations and organs taking the decisions.[69] This situation is in fact the reflection in law of what was discussed under the heading 'globalization and normative development'. In a globalizing world, demands for regulating issues of common interest arise. However, as such issues are being addressed, it is becoming apparent that existing decision-making processes are intimately linked to the inter-state normative pattern and not attuned to the common-interest normative pattern where actors other than states may be directly affected by decisions taken. As a result, demands for more inclusive and transparent decision-making processes and more accountable institutions arise. Such demands, due to the fact that they require the introduction of systemic change into the contemporary international legal system, are not easily accommodated by that system.

Democratic processes or procedures that are associated with the rule of law are not characteristic of existing international decision-making process.[70] As Brunnée has analyzed, with respect to the Climate Change regime, issues both of horizontal legitimacy – between states – and of vertical legitimacy – between states and civil society – arise.[71] While issues of horizontal and vertical legitimacy both will require

68 See, for example, text at and *supra* notes 23 and 24 and references in *supra* note 11.

69 See references in *supra* note 11.

70 See *e.g.*, Brunnée and Toope, *supra* note 5, Bodansky and Korhonene, *supra* note 11.

71 Brunnée, *supra* note 11.

changes in the international legal system, introducing increased vertical legitimacy will require changes in the secondary rules. In other words, introducing greater vertical legitimacy will require changes in the doctrines of the sources and the subjects of international law and, I submit, in the related concept of state-consent.

As I mentioned in my previous inaugural lecture, calls for the increased accountability of international organizations and other bodies have resulted in experimentation and exploration in the area of dispute settlement.[72] In this area several procedures have been established, some of which qualify as law-based forums, and some of which do not qualify as such. An example of the first type of procedure is the Optional Rules for Arbitration of Disputes Relating to Natural Resources/or the Environment, adopted by the Permanent Court of Arbitration[73] and which enable disputes between and among states, international organizations and private parties to be considered. An example of the second type of procedure is the World Bank Inspection Panel.[74] The Panel, although not qualifying as a court, applies the internal norms developed within the World Bank in a semi-judicial manner and translates the social relationship between the Bank and individuals and groups into a normative relationship. That relationship, according to most commentators, does not qualify as a legally relevant relationship in public international law for no other reason than that it does not fit the definition of a legal relationship in that system. This, however, is a rather circular argument. It is, moreover, from a legal policy point of view a dangerous argument, because it exempts, at least in a formal sense, such a procedure from rules of due process and from the principle that public power should be exercised subject to the rule of law. The discourse summarized here illustrates the difficulties involved in introducing vertical legitimacy in international law.

---

72 Ellen Hey, *Reflections on an International Environmental Court*, Kluwer Law International, 2000.

73 See the website of the Permanent Court of Arbitration http://www.pac-cpa.org.

74 Identical decisions of the International Bank for Reconstruction and Development (IBRD) and the International Development Association (IDA) were adopted on September 22, 1993, IBRD Res. 93-10 (1993) and IDA Res. 93-6 in respectively 34 ILM 520 (1995). In addition, the Executive Directors of the Bank in 1996 and 1999 adopted clarifications to the two afore-mentioned Resolutions, respectively entitled "Review of the Resolution Establishing the Inspectional Panel Clarifications of Certain Aspects" and "Conclusions of the Board's Second Review of the Inspection Panel". The decisions establishing the Panel, as well as the clarifications, are available from the website of the Panel http://www.inspectionpanel.org. Also see Ellen Hey, "The World Bank Inspection Panel: Towards the Recognition of a New Legally relevant Relationship in International Law," 2 *Hofstra Law and Policy Symposium* 1997, p. 61.

Understanding state-consent as consent to a process of normative development requires us to reexamine relevant decision-making processes in order to assess the legitimacy of decision-making processes and the accountability of the institutions involved in these processes. Similar arguments apply to compliance procedures under multilateral environmental agreements and have arisen in the framework of the procedures being developed under the Kyoto Protocol, where it is envisaged that the compliance commission will be able to take legally binding decisions.[75] Models of national administrative law may help us in understanding these developments.

I return to the International Criminal Court and the ongoing actions of the United States, but, in its wake, also other states, to limit the jurisdiction of that Court.[76] This situation very aptly illustrates the problems that may arise when the inter-state normative pattern and the common-interest normative pattern meet. Significantly, it also illustrates how issues of legitimacy may arise within the common-interest pattern.

Consent to the Statute of the International Criminal Court clearly is more aptly portrayed as consent to a process of normative development, a process in which the International Criminal Court will play a crucial role in the development of international criminal law. This role in many ways is likely to be similar to the role of the European Court of Human Rights in the development of human rights law in Europe. The bilateral agreements that the United States has and is in the process of concluding with other states clearly belong to the inter-state normative pattern.[77] In these agreements the United States and another state agree that they, absent the agreement of the state of nationality, will not surrender or transfer by any means persons to the International Criminal Court or to a third state, with the purpose of surrendering or transferring that person to the International Criminal Court. The interest of the international community in having an international criminal procedure that is complementary to national courts is thereby undermined. This situation raises questions regarding the compatibility of these agreements with the obligation of states-parties to the Statute, who are under an obligation to prosecute, or surrender suspects to the Court.[78] Moreover, the compatibility with the obligations of states-

---

75 See Brunnée, *supra* note 11.

76 See text at *supra* note 28 and thereafter.

77 See *supra* note 29.

78 Art. 1 *juncto* art. 17, Statute of the International Criminal Court.

signatories to the Statute of the International Criminal Court also arises. On the basis of article 18 of the Vienna Convention on the Law of Treaties, they are bound not to engage in acts contrary to the object and purpose of the Statute. In short, when the two patterns meet difficulties and uncertainties arise.

In considering the relationship between the Statute of the International Criminal Court and the resolution adopted by the Security Council,[79] a first element to note is that both the Statute and the decision-making process in the Security Council belong to the common-interest pattern of international law. The second noteworthy point in this respect is that the Security Council, as an institution within the common-interest pattern of law, by adopting the aforementioned resolution has raised questions about the legitimacy of the decision-making process within the common-interest normative pattern. This is because the resolution is inconsistent with a previous decision taken by that community, even if not by the Security Council itself.[80] Moreover, the decision results in inequality before the law between persons of different nationalities participating in military operations authorized by the Security Council. Furthermore, the decision creates a special position for military operations authorized by the Security Council,[81] as opposed to those engaged in for purposes of self-defense; the Security Council has thereby created a special position for its own operations and thus placed itself above the law. Needless to say, this development creates a situation that is not conducive to the introduction of the rule of law in international affairs and that raises questions about the legitimacy of the decision, the decision-making process and the organ involved, *i.e.*, the Security Council.[82]

Conclusions

Constructing state-consent as consent to a process, and more specifically as consent to a process aimed at normative development, the outcome of which is unknown at the time that consent is given, may help us in clarifying normative, including legal, development at the transnational level under the influence of globalization.

---

79 See *supra* note 30.

80 On the importance of consistency of decisions-taken see Brunnée and Toope, *supra* note 5.

81 *Ibid.*

82 Andrea Bianchi, "Ad-hocism and the Rule of Law," 13 *European Journal of International Law* 2002, p. 263.

As illustrated, constructing the concept of state-consent as consent to a process of normative development is not unproblematic in international law. It raises questions about the legitimacy of international decision-making processes and the accountability of the institutions involved and gives rise to demands for changes in the secondary rules of international law. As such changes are being introduced, systemic change is ongoing in the international legal system. This presents us, as teachers and lawyers, with a challenging environment. First, as teachers we probably find that a stable system is easier to teach than a systemically changing system, because, among other reasons, teaching the latter may require us to say "I do not know" – the source of all inspiration.[83] Second, as lawyers we generally have a predisposition in favor of stability because it enhances legal certainty, which we generally consider to be a good thing.

Due to the fact that our students will be working with a legal system that is in flux, I maintain that we have a duty to engage our students in a dialogue in which they are exposes to systemic change in the international legal system and can learn to work with that changing legal system. This means that we need to present them with a construct of the international legal system that not only encompasses the inter-state normative pattern, but one that presents the inter-state normative pattern as part of a broader story, a story that also includes the common-interest normative pattern and that is fraught with uncertainties. This essay is an attempt to illustrate how this broader story might be told with respect to one central element of the system of public international law – the concept of state-consent.

Acknowledgements

I thank the Board of Directors of the Erasmus University Rotterdam, and in particular the Rector Magnificus, Professor Jan van Bemmel, and the Board of the Faculty of Law, and in particular its Dean, Professor Jaap de Zwaan, for entrusting me with the Chair of Public International Law.

Jaap, I thank you for making my re-entry into the faculty a very smooth one and for being a very supportive colleague.

---

[83] Wislawa Szymborska, "De Dichter en de Wereld," (The Poet and the World), speech delivered upon the acceptance of the Nobel Prize for Literature, 7 December 1996, *Einde en Begin, Gedichten 1975-1997* (End and Beginning, Poems 1975-1997), Meulenhoff, 1999, p. 291, p. 293.

Colleagues at the Faculty of Law, I thank you for the fact that from the first day of my appointment you have made me feel more than welcome in your midst.

I am particularly happy with the manner in which, within the Capacity Group Public Law, we approach the teaching responsibilities that we share.

Professor Roel de Lange, I found our weekly classes on human rights law, last semester, to be very inspiring indeed. They constitute a route that I certainly hope to pursue both in teaching and research responsibilities, also with other colleagues.

Members of the Department of Public International Law, Juan Amaya-Castro, Gerhard Anders, Math Noortmann and Miklos Redner, you have made me feel most welcome. While I had worked with each of you previously and we all knew each other, I had also during the year and a half prior to my appointment taken some distance from the department. This makes my smooth return in your midst all the more remarkable. Thank you! I trust that we will continue to work together with the object of excelling in our various teaching and research endeavors. I am familiar with your jokes about my concerns related to the 'group'; however, I remain convinced that our strength as a group is that we represent a variety of critical approaches to international law, approaches that we integrate into our teaching and research responsibilities. I look forward to our continued cooperation.

Math, you more than kept things going at the department in sometimes difficult times. Looking towards the future, I express the hope and the confidence that in close cooperation amongst ourselves and with others, we will further develop teaching and research in the area of public international law at Erasmus.

Gerhard, Juan and Miklos, each of you has shared in teaching and other responsibilities at the department and those responsibilities in the past have gone beyond what could reasonably be expected of you. Your main focus now can and should be on your research endeavors. That is the way it should be and I will do my utmost to keep it that way.

Professor Albert Koers, you taught me many valuable lessons in the field of international lawboth as a teacher and as a researcher. I will do my utmost to live up to those lessons and, in particular, to endeavor to share with my students a very valuable lesson that you taught me, i.e. that 'I do not know' is the source of all inspiration.[84]

---

[84] *Id.*

I thank Olaf Kwast and Andre Noort, my successive student-assistants, for helping me with the gathering of the material for this essay.

I thank Philomene Verlaan for editing the manuscript of this essay, Annebeth Rosenboom, at Kluwer, for facilitating its publication, Steve Lambley for typesetting and making the cover layout and Ed Brandon for the photographic work.

I thank Mi Desmedt for once again allowing me to select one of her inspiring works of art for the cover of this essay.

Last but by no means least, I address the participants in my classes and whose initial steps in legal research I supervise: my students. It is my aim as expressed in this lecture to offer you insights that will enable you to work with a systemically changing legal system. I expect you to be critical, not only because that is what you will need to be when you are working in practice, but also in order to keep me sharp. I have and will continue to have a lot to learn and explore, you can help me in that endeavor and the journey will be all the more pleasant if we undertake it together. Although classes are often extremely large, I hope that you and I will also under those circumstances find opportunities to discuss the interests that we share.

www.ingramcontent.com/pod-product-compliance
Ingram Content Group UK Ltd.
Pitfield, Milton Keynes, MK11 3LW, UK
UKHW041335110926
15112UKWH00015B/44

9 789041 120144